Teen Guide to
MANAGING
STRESS AND
ANXIETY

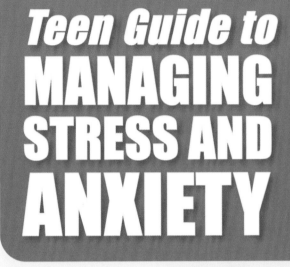

Barbara Sheen

ReferencePoint
Press

San Diego, CA

© 2022 ReferencePoint Press, Inc.
Printed in the United States

For more information, contact:
ReferencePoint Press, Inc.
PO Box 27779
San Diego, CA 92198
www.ReferencePointPress.com

LIBRARY OF CONGRESS CATALOGING-IN-PUBLICATION DATA

Names: Sheen, Barbara, author.
Title: Teen guide to managing stress and anxiety / by Barbara Sheen.
Description: San Diego, CA : ReferencePoint Press, Inc., 2021. | Includes
  bibliographical references and index.
Identifiers: LCCN 2021000557 (print) | LCCN 2021000558 (ebook) | ISBN
  9781678200947 (library binding) | ISBN 9781678200954 (ebook)
Subjects: LCSH: Anxiety in adolescence--Juvenile literature. | Stress in
  adolescence--Juvenile literature. | Worry in adolescence--Juvenile
  literature.
Classification: LCC BF724.3.A57 S53 2021 (print) | LCC BF724.3.A57
  (ebook) | DDC 155.5/1246--dc23
LC record available at https://lccn.loc.gov/2021000557
LC ebook record available at https://lccn.loc.gov/2021000558

CONTENTS

A Stressful Time

Max is an eighteen-year-old college freshman. Like so many other people, he experienced a lot of stress between 2019 and 2020. During his senior year of high school, between keeping up with his schoolwork, being a member of the varsity hockey team, working part time, doing household chores, and socializing with his friends, his schedule was jam-packed. Plus there were college applications that had to be filled out perfectly, followed by waiting and worrying over where he would be accepted. If this was not nerve-racking enough, in the spring of 2020 the COVID-19 pandemic struck, and Max's already stressful world was turned upside down. The pandemic caused his school to shut down. Max spent his final semester of high school on Zoom. He missed his friends and felt socially isolated and disconnected. He reasoned that his life would return to normal when he went off to college in the fall. But that did not happen. With the pandemic still raging, Max attended college from his bedroom via remote learning. This was not the college experience he had been looking forward to.

In fact, nothing was the way it should have been. When his parents and older brother contracted the virus, he was forced to isolate himself even further. And he worried about losing family members to the virus. Max felt frustrated and depressed. He started getting unexplained stomachaches. He was not where he wanted to be, and his future was filled with uncertainty.

Max did not know it, but his stomachaches and negative feelings were caused by stress overload. Lots of teens share Max's feelings. Normal stressors, combined with pandemic-induced stress, have taken their toll on young people.

Being a Teenager Is Not Easy

Being a teenager is not easy. It can be an emotional roller coaster. Even in the best of times, the teen years are filled with all sorts of changes and uncertainties. This can lead to feeling irritated, fearful, sad, and overwhelmed—sometimes all at the same time. Physically, teenage bodies are changing. Fluctuating hormone levels involved in physical growth and sexual development can cause frequent mood swings. Teens tend to be more impulsive and emotional than adults because the part of the brain that controls reasoning and emotional responses is still developing. Dealing with acne, growth spurts, and sexual impulses—as well as with parental, peer, academic, and social media pressures—does not help. And if all of this is not enough, there's bullying, racial injustice, a pandemic, climate change, and other social issues to worry about.

It is no wonder teens are stressed out. As singer/rapper Willow Smith, who struggles with anxiety, explains, "Anything could happen. . . . I think everyone has a fear of just not knowing what's going to happen in the future, not knowing if you're on the right path, not knowing if you're making the right choices."[1] Indeed, a 2020 poll sponsored by the National 4-H Council of fifteen hundred teenagers found that 65 percent of respondents felt anxious or depressed due to uncertainty about the future.

> "I think everyone has a fear of just not knowing what's going to happen in the future, not knowing if you're on the right path, not knowing if you're making the right choices."[1]
>
> —Willow Smith, singer/rapper

A Common Problem

Clearly, the teen years are a stressful period in a person's life, especially during a pandemic, when life is far from normal. Whereas stress is a natural part of life that can help us survive when faced with danger or help motivate us to get things done, too much stress can be harmful. When stress becomes overwhelming, it can turn into anxiety. Anxiety is an overreaction to stress. It causes persistent worry and feelings of dread, which can negatively affect a person's life.

Indeed, stress, stress overload and anxiety are common mental health issues in young people. A 2018 poll conducted by the social network After School asked more than thirty-five thousand teenagers how often they felt stressed. Almost 45 percent responded that they felt stressed all of the time. Two years later the COVID-19 pandemic intensified teen stress. In a 2020 survey of more than two thousand students conducted by Active Minds, an organization that supports mental health awareness, 87 percent of the respondents reported experiencing stress and anxiety.

Filled with all sorts of changes and uncertainties, teen life can be an emotional roller coaster.

Becoming Resilient

Excess stress over extended time periods can affect a person's physical and mental health. Some teens turn to drugs, alcohol, risky behavior, or suicide attempts as a way to escape from the tension they are under. This type of destructive behavior only makes things worse. Fortunately, there are many steps you can take to keep stress and anxiety at bay. In fact, learning to manage stress makes you more resilient and better able to face life's minor and major disasters. As wellness coach Elizabeth Scott explains, "Resilient people tend to view life's difficulties as challenges and respond accordingly with action, rather than with fear, self-pity, blame or a victim mentality."[2]

Developing resiliency does not happen overnight. Stress management is an ongoing process. But when stress and anxiety seem overwhelming, it is important to know that you, and not stress, are in the driver's seat.

> "Resilient people tend to view life's difficulties as challenges and respond accordingly with action, rather than with fear, self-pity, blame or a victim mentality."[2]
>
> —Elizabeth Scott, wellness coach

CHAPTER ONE

Not Just an Emotional Issue

Sixteen-year-old Sonya was frantically struggling to complete an assignment in biology class when she started feeling strange. "My face got really hot, and my whole body felt paralyzed," she recalls. "It seemed like the walls were closing in on me."[3]

Sonya did not know what was happening. She was very frightened and went to the school counselor for help. She learned that she'd had a panic attack and that her symptoms were caused by overwhelming anxiety. She also learned that lots of teens were experiencing these feelings.

Since that time, Sonya has learned a lot about stress and anxiety, as well as how to cope with the problems they can cause. Learning about stress and anxiety, their effects on the body, and what specific events triggers stress in you personally are important steps in managing your response. As Karen Young, an Australian psychologist and author of the website Hey Sigmund, explains:

Understanding why anxiety feels the way it does will be one of your greatest tools in managing it. Think of it like this. Imagine being in a dark room that is full of "stuff." When you walk around in the dark, you're going to bump into things. You're going to scrape, bruise and maybe drop a few choice words. Turn on the light though, and those things are still there, but now you can navigate your way around them. No more bumps. No more scrapes.[4]

What Is Stress?

Stress is the body's physical, emotional, and mental reaction to a perceived threat. Such threats are known as triggers or stressors. Most stressors are related to specific events and demands in our lives that seem difficult to cope with. Stress can be mild, moderate, or severe and can be beneficial or harmful, depending on the amount of stress and the circumstances. Feeling stressed before competing in a race, trying out for a team, or taking a big test, for example, can be beneficial. The physiological effect stress has on the body makes you feel stronger, more alert, and more energetic, which can enhance your performance. Nebraska school psychologist Diane Marti explains that when you are stressed, "your nervous system clicks on like a button, and boom! Your heart starts pumping faster and you get a burst of energy that helps you get things done."[5]

Normally, the physiological effects of stress are short term. When that big test or other stressful event is over, you put it out of your thoughts and your body relaxes. However, if you are being bombarded by multiple stressors, or you are dealing with a persistent stressor such as being bullied or a seriously ill loved one, your body does not get a chance to relax. As a result, you feel overpowered by stress. This is known as stress overload.

Long-Term Stress Overload

When stress overload continues for at least six weeks, it can develop into anxiety. Anxiety is a chronic condition categorized by

"Understanding why anxiety feels the way it does will be one of your greatest tools in managing it."[4]

—Karen Young, psychologist and author of the website Hey Sigmund out-of-control fear and worry, even when there is no identifiable reason for these feelings. Anxiety makes you feel nervous and panicky. It can interfere with your day-to-day life and lower your self-esteem. When anxiety takes over, it is not unusual for individuals to doubt themselves, procrastinate, avoid people or social events, and have problems making decisions.

Persistent worry about what might happen in the future and how your actions will affect the future are typical symptoms of anxiety. This fear can put your mind into an anxiety loop of what-ifs that can be emotionally paralyzing. Singer-songwriter Julia Michaels, as an example, started having problems with anxiety when she was eighteen.

> I'd just signed my first publishing deal, and I felt so much pressure to perform that it sent my mind and body down something that felt like a never-ending spiral. . . . I became afraid of everything. Going out. Eating. Driving. Writing. My life became a string of what-ifs. What if I eat this and I'm allergic to it? What if I'm driving and get in an accident? What happens if I stop moving? I became consumed. I didn't know who I was anymore. I had completely isolated myself—even from the things I loved.[6]

Panic attacks, which are frightening episodes that occur suddenly and without warning, are also caused by anxiety. A panic attack feels similar to a heart attack. During a panic attack, individuals sweat and shake, have difficulty breathing, feel dizzy, or feel like they are choking, among other alarming symptoms.

On average, panic attacks last about ten minutes and typically occur only a few times in a person's lifetime. Frequent panic attacks are a symptom of a panic disorder. A panic disorder is a type of anxiety disorder. Anxiety disorders are mental conditions. There are many kinds of anxiety disorders. Each has specific symptoms, but all cause persistent and intense anxiety. Anxiety disorders include but are not limited to panic disorder; generalized

Panic attacks occur suddenly and without warning, and have symptoms such as difficulty breathing, dizziness, and choking sensations.

anxiety disorder, which is characterized by excessive worry about almost everything; and social anxiety disorder, which is characterized by fear and worry related to social situations. Obsessive-compulsive disorder, a condition in which people are plagued by unwanted thoughts and perform compulsive acts in an effort to quell these thoughts, and post-traumatic stress disorder (PTSD) are other anxiety disorders. The causes of anxiety disorders are not totally understood. Research suggests anxiety disorders are caused by a combination of genetics, brain chemistry, and traumatic events. Excess anxiety may also be involved in the development of an anxiety disorder, according to the Mayo Clinic.

Fight or Flight

When people are very stressed or anxious, they feel jittery and nervous. Their heart beats faster, their breathing becomes rapid and shallow, their mouth becomes dry, and they feel like they have butterflies in their stomach. This is because stress and anxiety have a strong physiological effect on the body. They activate a primitive response known as the fight-or-flight response or the acute stress response, which puts the body on high alert so that it can respond to a perceived threat. This response protected early humans from real dangers like an attack by a wild animal but is not as helpful in dealing with modern stressors like misplacing your keys. The problem is, your body responds in the same way to either event.

The fight-or-flight response begins in the brain. When the amygdala, a part of the brain that regulates emotions, identifies a threat, it immediately sets off an alarm. It signals the body to release adrenaline, cortisol, and other stress hormones that prepare the body for action. As a result, your heart rate, blood pressure, and blood sugar level increase, which gives you extra energy but also makes you feel on edge. At the same time, oxygen and blood are diverted from your extremities and sent to the muscles and vital organs. While this gives you added strength, it can also cause you to feel dizzy. In addition, your digestion slows and stomach

Stress and anxiety can be caused by external triggers such as a looming deadline, or by internal triggers such as the inability to accept uncertainty.

acids are released, giving you indigestion. And to keep your body from overheating, you sweat. Besides these physical responses, as stress hormones course through the brain, they cause mental changes, which make you feel confused, affect your ability to make decisions, or make you freeze up with inaction.

The fight-or-flight response can save your life if you are being attacked, but it is an over-the-top reaction to stress caused by a pop quiz or something you saw on social media. And if you do not understand what is happening to you, it can be quite frightening. "The thing is," explains Catherine M. Pittman, a psychologist and professor of psychology at Saint Mary's College in Indiana, "your amygdala can't distinguish between an immediate danger (like having a gun pointed at you) and perceived danger (like knowing the world is full of forces that threaten your safety)—it activates the same responses either way."[7]

Moreover, even thinking about a stressful event can activate the response, as can watching a scary movie. Plus, if you are dealing with multiple or long-term stressors, it can be difficult to shut the response down. Consequently, your body does not get a chance to rest and recuperate. Remaining in a heightened state of alert causes stress hormones to build up and puts the body out of balance. This can make you feel even more stressed and negatively affect your physical and mental health. In fact, over time, it lessens your body's ability to fight off infection.

> "Your amygdala can't distinguish between an immediate danger (like having a gun pointed at you) and perceived danger (like knowing the world is full of forces that threaten your safety)—it activates the same responses either way."[7]
>
> —Catherine M. Pittman, psychologist and professor of psychology at Saint Mary's College

Internal and External Stressors

Stress and anxiety are brought on by external and internal triggers or stressors. External stressors are rooted in external events such as cyberbullying, a looming deadline, or a news report. Internal

Although spending time on social media can be fun, it can also trigger stress. According to an article on the website Verywell Family:

> Teens often feel emotionally invested in their social media accounts. Not only do they feel pressure to respond quickly online, but they also feel pressure to have perfect photos and well-written posts, all of which can cause a great deal of anxiety. In fact, some studies have found that the larger a teen's social circle online the more anxiety they feel about keeping up with everything online. Additionally, if teens commit a faux pas online, this also can be an extreme source of anxiety. Many teens, especially girls, are prone to worry about what others might think of them and how they will respond when they see them next. Then factor in cyberbullying, slut-shaming, and other mean online behaviors and you can see why social media is a very real source of anxiety for many teens.
>
> Therefore, if you identify social media as one of your stressors, limiting the time you spend on social media can help you manage your feelings.

Sherri Gordon, "5 Ways Social Media Affects Teen Mental Health," Verywell Family, July 13, 2020. www.verywell family.com.

stressors are rooted in stress-inducing thoughts or behaviors. The need to be perfect, the inability to accept uncertainty or lack of control, and various fears like fear of flying or public speaking are just a few examples of internal stressors. Both internal and external stressors can be positive or negative. Being criticized on social media, an argument with your parents, responsibilities at home, or ending a romantic relationship are examples of negative stressors. Getting married, starting a new job or new school, or learning something new, among other things, are positive stressors. Whether internal or external, positive or negative, all stressors can evoke the fight-or-flight response.

Stress triggers are also very personal and subjective. What causes you to feel stressed may have little or no effect on your best friend. Attending a social event where you are surrounded by strangers may send you into full panic mode, for instance, but have no impact on your more outgoing pal. Similarly, everyone reacts to stress differently. Your age, life experiences, and family influence what stresses you and how you respond to stress. For example, since parents serve as role models, the way your parents respond to stress influences your response to stress. If your parents tend to overreact to minor events, you probably have learned to respond in a similar manner. Your age and experiences also impact what triggers stress in you and how you handle it. When you were a toddler, being separated from your parents may have caused you great stress, and you probably reacted by crying or screaming. This particular stress trigger, however, probably has less impact on you today, mainly because your life experiences tell you that the separation is temporary.

Identifying Triggers Helps Us Cope

Since everyone's stressors are different, it is important to identify your stressors. Knowing what triggers stress in you and how you respond can help you effectively deal with stress before it becomes overwhelming. This is not as simple as it sounds. Although identifying major stressors, such as the death of a pet or moving to a new city, is easy, it is more difficult to pinpoint smaller stressors. But you can do it.

One of the most effective ways to identify stress triggers and how you respond to them is by keeping a stress diary. This involves keeping a record of each time you felt stressed, the level of stress you felt, the cause of your stress, how you reacted physically and emotionally, what you did to relieve your stress, and how well this worked. Since you may not always know the exact stressor, it is okay to guess. Over time, you should be able to pinpoint patterns, which can help you identify specific sources of your stress and become more able to manage your response. For instance, if you find that being around a certain person causes you high levels of stress, you can lessen the power of this stressor by limiting how much time you spend with that person. If this is not possible because the person is someone you must be around—such as a teacher, coworker, family member, or teammate—you can still manage the stress this person causes you by using techniques that have helped you relieve stress in other situations. When you analyze your stress diary, you may find that distracting yourself for a short time by working on a hobby, going for a walk, listening to music, or shooting hoops, for example, helps you manage your response to stress. Actress Millie Bobby Brown, who has struggled with anxiety for most of her life, uses a number of distractions to manage stress. She says, "When I'm having a bad day or I'm feeling very anxious . . . I have learned to manage it in ways that a lot of people learn to manage things like breathing exercises or distracting your mind and my hobbies help distract me from being anxious. Driving takes my anxiety away, actually. I thought it would heighten it. I just don't think about anything [when driving]."[8]

Learning a new skill is one positive way of dealing with the stress of being socially isolated.

Although avoiding toxic people can help you manage stress, avoidance is not always a healthy way to cope with stress. Not going to school or work, not attending social events, or not working on an assignment to avoid stress can negatively impact the quality of your life. It can cause you to isolate yourself or procrastinate to the point that you fail to get things done, which in the long run will increase stress. As author and clinical psychologist Earl Hipp writes:

> Think of avoidance as distractions carried to the extreme—like when watching a little TV becomes watching every night for hours and hours. It's when a simple activity starts to take up more and more of your time and energy and causes you to put off dealing with things you're worried about or don't want to do. Unfortunately, this can lead to a vicious circle of behavior. . . . For example, hanging out with friends is great and can be an effective way to de-stress. But spending all your time with friends—day and night, in person or online—to distract yourself from difficulties at home or school can become a stress-generating and self-destructive pattern of avoidance.

Earl Hipp, *Fighting Invisible Tigers*. Minneapolis, MN: Free Spirit, 2019, p.13.

Change Your Thoughts

Changing your thoughts can also help you manage stress. Once you have identified your stressors, when you are faced with these stressors you can lessen their impact through positive self-talk. Positive self-talk involves mentally saying optimistic and positive things to and about yourself instead of dwelling on negative thoughts. For instance, reminding yourself that you are smart and typically get good grades can lessen the stress an upcoming exam has on you. Similarly, when faced with any challenging event, recalling stressful situations that you handled successfully helps remind you of how capable you really are. As a result, you are less likely to feel stressed by new challenges and more ready to meet them head-on. Or when a negative person stresses you by tearing you down, whether in person or on social media, mentally ticking off your strengths can build your confidence and lessen the effect this person has on you. "Being your own biggest support team is so important, too," Brown explains. "I rely on myself to give myself self-love, because that's just literally the only way I can. I tell myself, 'Wow. I did good in that,' and I have to give myself love because that's important. Everyone has to empower themselves."[9]

Changing your attitude toward stressors is also useful, especially when you are dealing with situations that you have little control over. If, for example, the social isolation and uncertainty of the COVID-19 pandemic has had you feeling sad and anxious, try to look at the situation in a more positive light. Try viewing it as a chance to reconnect with your family or an opportunity do some of the alone things you have not had time for in the past, like learning a new skill such as photography, knitting, or playing guitar. And try to put the situation in perspective. Accepting that you cannot control everything lessens stress and helps you move on.

Indeed, understanding stress and the way it impacts you personally is an important step in managing it. As author and businessperson Arianna Huffington writes, "When we know ourselves—the sources of our stress, how we respond, and what actions help us recharge—we're far better able to minimize the damage. We can't eliminate stress, but we can learn to manage it."[10]

CHAPTER TWO

Fighting Stress with a Healthy Lifestyle

Rizza Bermio-Gonzalez is a young woman who has struggled with anxiety since she was in middle school. She is also a coauthor of *Treating Anxiety*, a blog featured on Healthy-Place. In one of her posts, she recalls how stressed she felt while she was a student and how her lifestyle impacted her stress: "My anxiety was at an all-time high. I was juggling work, school, family. . . . I was extremely overwhelmed. . . . During the time, I ate quite a bit of processed and fast food, and I drank a lot of coffee and energy drinks. . . . I also often found that the more I ate like this, the more I felt anxious, moody, and exhausted."[11]

Since that time, Bermio-Gonzalez has changed her eating habits, which has helped her manage her anxiety. Research has shown that living a healthy lifestyle—eating a nutritious diet, staying hydrated, getting adequate sleep, and being physically active—is vital to effectively managing stress.

Healthy Eating

Eating a balanced, nutrient-rich diet and avoiding bad dietary habits are very important strategies for managing stress. A diet that is rich in protein, complex carbohydrates, fiber, vitamins, and minerals and contains moderate amounts of good fats has a positive effect on how you look and feel. This is because the food you eat fuels your mind and body. Protein-rich foods such as meat, fish, poultry, eggs, nuts, beans, and seeds repair and build muscles and cells and help brain cells communicate with each other. The latter enables you to concentrate and think clearly. In addition to these benefits, eggs, fish, chicken, turkey, and beans contain tryptophan. Tryptophan is an amino acid, or organic compound, that is connected to the production of serotonin, a chemical that helps regulate mood and sleep and relieve anxiety. Other tryptophan-rich foods include bananas, oats, and cheese.

Eating plenty of fruits and vegetables also helps manage stress. Fruits and vegetables are rich in vitamins and minerals that help battle disease and reduce inflammation. Inflammation is your body's response to illness and injury. Anxiety and stress generate inflammation, which, if it goes on too long or occurs unnecessarily, can damage the body. Fruits and vegetables also contain fiber, which helps your digestive system function efficiently. This is especially helpful when the fight-or-flight response slows digestion. Additionally, potatoes, sweet potatoes, broccoli, bananas, cantaloupe, and dried apricots provide the body with potassium, a mineral that has a calming effect on the body. Dried apricots are also rich in magnesium, a mineral that helps regulate blood pressure. In fact, research published in 2020 in the International Journal of Environmental Research and Public Health links a diet rich in protein, vitamins, and minerals to improved mental health.

Good and Bad Choices

Other foods that contain probiotics also have a beneficial effect on stress and anxiety. These foods include but are not limited to yogurt, kefir, sauerkraut, pickles, miso, and some types of cheese, such as mozzarella, cheddar, and gouda. Probiotics are beneficial bacteria that improve digestive health. Exactly how probiotics lessen anxiety is not entirely clear. However, several studies sug-

gest that probiotics reduce cortisol levels and combat digestive problems, which can be caused by stress or trigger stress. Therefore, adding these foods to your diet is a good idea.

Other foods are not as helpful. Many processed foods are detrimental to controlling stress. These include most fast-food meals and processed meat and cheese, as well as margarine, crackers, white bread, pastries, and chips. When food is processed, artificial ingredients are added to the food, and nutrients and fiber are destroyed. Consequently, processed food is typically low in essential nutrients.

Sugary processed foods like pastries, candy, energy drinks, and soft drinks are not helpful, either. They contain few nutrients and high levels of simple carbohydrates in the form of sugar. These foods give you a brief burst of energy that leaves you feeling tired, moody, and irritable. Complex carbohydrates found in whole grains, nuts, brown rice, and beans are a better choice. They provide you with long-lasting energy and have a calming effect on the body.

Besides being loaded with sugar, most soft drinks and energy drinks, as well as coffee and many teas, contain caffeine. Caffeine is a drug that provides users with a temporary boost of energy. It affects the brain and body much like the fight-or-flight response. Even a small amount of caffeine stimulates the brain to release stress hormones, while it hinders the absorption of other chemicals that calm the body. Caffeine raises heart rate, blood pressure, and brain activity, making people feel agitated. After the effects wear off, users may feel tired, depressed, and stressed. In an effort to counteract these feelings, many individuals consume more caffeine, which causes the brain to release even more stress hormones. In fact, too much caffeine can lead to panic attacks. As wellness counselor Elizabeth Scott writes, "If you ingest high levels of caffeine, you may feel your mood soar and plummet, leaving you craving more caffeine to make it soar again, causing you to lose sleep, suffer health consequences, and feel more stress."[12]

The way a person eats can also help with managing stress. Gobbling down food and eating on the run can cause indigestion, which can induce stress or worsen stress-related digestive issues. Eating slowly and chewing thoroughly aids digestion and the absorption of nutrients. It prevents too much air from getting into the stomach, which can cause bloating and gas—two stressful occurrences. As Oregon author and mental health counselor Tanya J. Peterson explains, "Food is important in anxiety reduction and stress management. You can make a positive difference in your mental health and wellbeing by being intentional about what you eat and how you eat it."[13]

"If you ingest high levels of caffeine, you may feel your mood soar and plummet, leaving you craving more caffeine to make it soar again, causing you to lose sleep, suffer health consequences, and feel more stress."[12]

—Elizabeth Scott, wellness counselor

22

It can be difficult to tell whether you are getting a nutrient-rich diet. Looking at the colors of the food on your plate can be a big help. The more colors on your plate, the more nutrients you are getting. For example, a meal that includes a green salad with red tomatoes, a piece of orange salmon, brown rice, a slice of dark whole grain bread that you dip in olive oil, and blueberries or purple grapes for dessert is loaded with essential nutrients and has stress-relieving properties. A snack of nutrient-rich smoothie made from a mix of frozen fruit, yogurt, milk or water, and a teaspoon of honey has similar benefits.

Determining how much food you should eat can also be puzzling. The number of calories teens need each day depends on how active they are. On average, teenage boys require 2,800 calories a day, while teenage girls require 2,300 calories. To help you find out how many calories and nutrients you are getting, check food labels. They list the number of calories and amount of nutrients per serving.

Drink Water

Staying hydrated by drinking plenty of water is another way to manage stress and anxiety. Water cleanses your body and helps keep you healthy. It lubricates the joints and is vital for digestion. It also flushes toxins and waste out of the body through urination and helps regulate body temperature through perspiration, among other functions. About 60 percent of your body weight is made up of water. Keeping the correct balance of water in your body is essential to good health. If you use more water than you take in, it negatively impacts the way you feel. In fact, dehydration increases cortisol levels, which is one reason the symptoms of mild dehydration closely mirror those of stress and anxiety. Symptoms of mild dehydration include dry mouth, indigestion, headaches, dizziness, irritability, moodiness, and an inability to concentrate or think clearly. The results of a 2012 study reported in the *Journal of the American College of Nutrition* found that decreasing the balance of water in the body by as little as 2 percent impairs mental performance.

Making matters worse, in some cases dehydration can trigger a panic attack. Moreover, because stress and anxiety cause

Staying well hydrated by drinking plenty of water is another way to manage stress and anxiety.

excess perspiration, stress can lead to dehydration. Therefore, it is especially important to drink water when you are feeling stressed. As nutrition expert Amanda Carlson explains, "Staying in a good hydrated status can keep your stress levels down. When you don't give your body the fluids it needs, you're putting stress on it, and it's going to respond to that."[14]

One way to tell whether you are drinking enough water is by checking the color of your urine. Dark yellow urine is an indication of dehydration, while pale, almost clear urine is a good indicator that you are getting enough water. And if you do not like the way water tastes, you can make it more flavorful by adding a slice of lemon or lime, a watermelon chunk, or a cucumber slice.

> "Staying in a good hydrated status can keep your stress levels down. When you don't give your body the fluids it needs, you're putting stress on it, and it's going to respond to that."[14]
>
> —Amanda Carlson, nutrition expert

Getting Sufficient Sleep

A number of studies have determined that many teenagers do not get sufficient sleep. Teens need 9 hours of sleep each night but on average get about 7.4 hours. And because teens lead such busy lives, many get less than that. Sleep is essential for good physical and emotional health. While you sleep, your brain is active, repairing and replacing damaged cells; directing the release of hormones, including lowering cortisol levels; and processing the day's events, among other recuperative tasks. A good night's sleep enables you to think clearly and cope with whatever happens the next day. In contrast, lack of sleep makes you feel unwell. And it makes you more vulnerable to stress. Sixteen-year-old Sophie has felt the effects of inadequate sleep. She explains, "I've had headaches for two weeks straight and felt dizzy or dehydrated. I think anxiety is also worse when you don't sleep, and I've had shaking."[15]

What's more, the physiological effect of anxiety and stress can make it difficult to fall asleep. By practicing healthy habits that promote sleep, you can help counteract this effect. Establishing a sleep routine, for example, helps signal the brain that it is time to wind down for sleep. Such a routine includes making time to relax before going to bed, as well as having a fixed bedtime. Although it may be tempting, try not to watch a scary or disturbing movie, drink caffeinated beverages, or eat a heavy or spicy meal before bedtime, since these activities stimulate rather than relax the body. Instead, to calm your mind and body, consider taking a warm bath, listening to soothing music, or drinking a cup of warm milk or chamomile tea. Chamomile is an herb that contains substances that have relaxant properties, while milk and other dairy products contain tryptophan, which promotes sleep.

Keeping your bedroom cool and dark is also conducive to sleep. A sleep mask can help if you cannot get the room dark enough. Restricting the use of electronic devices such as cell phones, tablets, and computers close to bedtime is important, too. The bright light these devices emit stimulates the brain and disrupts the release of melatonin, a hormone that facilitates sleep.

Indeed, limiting nighttime use of social media has other benefits that can improve sleep. A 2019 British study looked at teen use of social media and the effect it has on sleep. According to the study, more than one in five teens spend five or more hours a day on social media. And, those teens that spend the most time on social media go to sleep later and have poorer sleep patterns than those who use social media less. Exposure to gossip, rumors, and contentious discussions right before going to bed is likely to create stress and disrupt sleep. Plus, a lot of teens have difficulty getting off social media because they do not want to miss anything. So instead of sleeping and letting the brain rest, they allow social media to take over their lives.

Exercise Is Important

Physical activity is another healthy lifestyle choice and a wonderful stress buster. Not only does physical activity strengthen the muscles, heart, lungs, and immune system, it has a positive effect on the mind and emotions. Exercise and other physical activities cause the body to produce endorphins, chemicals that relax the body and brain and give you a feeling of overall well-being. In addition, physical activity allows you to use up stress hormones that continue to circulate through your body due to stress overload and anxiety. Former First Lady Michelle Obama credits exercise with helping her handle stress. She says, "If I'm ever feeling tense or stressed or like I'm about to have a meltdown, I'll put on my iPod and head to the gym or out on a bike ride. Exercise is really important to me—it's therapeutic."[16]

Some gentle forms of exercise like yoga, tai chi, and qi gong are especially

"If I'm ever feeling tense or stressed or like I'm about to have a meltdown, I'll put on my iPod and head to the gym or out on a bike ride. Exercise is really important to me—it's therapeutic."[16]

—Michelle Obama, former First Lady

26

Drinking alcohol, taking drugs, and smoking or chewing tobacco are not part of a healthy lifestyle. These substances not only damage your health, they are not helpful in relieving stress. Yet according to a number of studies conducted by the National Center on Addiction and Substance Abuse at Columbia University, teens who are highly stressed are 50 percent more likely to abuse these substances than teens who are under low stress.

Using alcohol, drugs, or tobacco to calm your mind and body brings only temporary relief. Ultimately, these substances worsen the effects of stress. They expose the body to chemicals that make it very difficult to think clearly, cause the heart and lungs to work harder, stress the brain, and stimulate the release of stress hormones. Moreover, long-term use of these substances can make users more sensitive to stress.

calming. These practices focus on connecting your body and mind. They train you to detach from your thoughts and shift your attention onto your breathing, the position of your body, and the present moment, skills that are quite useful in managing anxious thoughts. In addition, practicing yoga has been shown to raise the brain's level of gamma-aminobutyric acid (GABA), a chemical that blocks the brain from transmitting stress-related messages to the rest of the body. In fact, most antianxiety medications stimulate the production of GABA, since people with anxiety disorders appear to have lower-than-average levels of the chemical. Conversely, high levels of GABA have been linked to feeling happy and relaxed.

Yoga also involves stretching. Gentle stretching—whether as a part of yoga practice, as a warm-up or cool-down to other types of exercise, or alone—reduces muscle tension, which helps release stress. When you are feeling stressed, taking a moment to perform a few revitalizing stretches that target the neck, shoulders, and lower back are particularly relaxing. Shoulder shrugs, for instance, relieve tension in the shoulders and neck. To get maximum stress relief, it is best to hold a stretch for about fifteen seconds without bouncing.

Gentle exercise such as yoga helps raise levels of gamma-aminobutyric acid (GABA), a chemical that blocks the brain from transmitting stress-related messages to the rest of the body.

Do What You Like

If these gentle forms of exercise do not appeal to you, that does not mean you cannot reap the stress-reducing benefits of exercise. Any form of physical activity is a stress buster. The key is finding activities that you enjoy. Playing sports, flying a kite, jumping on a trampoline, dancing, or walking all help relieve stress. In fact, according to the Anxiety and Depression Association of America, some studies suggest that a ten-minute walk can restore calm and reduce stress and anxiety.

Or maybe you prefer boxing and other martial arts. These are great ways to get rid of pent-up stress and intense emotions. Hitting a punching bag or sparring with a partner allows you to release the anger and frustration that stress and anxiety can cause. The key is to do whatever suits your personality and makes you feel good. If you like being part of a group, you can enroll in an exercise class or join a team. Even during a pandemic, there are online Zoom classes that let you be part of a group. Or if you need time alone, you can choose a solo activity like skipping rope, swimming, jogging, or weight training. Swimming in particular can be especially calming since being submerged in water has a soothing effect on the mind and body.

The US government recommends that teenagers get sixty minutes of moderate to vigorous exercise daily or, at minimum, thirty minutes three times a week. However, an American Psychological Association survey found that 20 percent of teens exercise once a week or less. If you fall into this category and cannot seem to commit to exercise, even small things that get you moving can help you manage stress. For instance, making small changes in your lifestyle like taking the stairs instead of an elevator have big benefits when it comes to controlling stress. And activities like cleaning your room, shoveling snow, playing the drums, doing yardwork, shopping, and playing catch with your siblings count as physical activities. Even doing a few jumping jacks causes the release of endorphins and other chemicals that make you feel mellower. So get started. The results are worth the effort.

CHAPTER THREE

Relax and Recharge

Jackie is a teen who has been dealing with anxiety since she was a child. After her father suddenly died, her anxiety level soared, and she did not know how to deal with it. Everything seemed to upset her. She felt tense and jittery most of the time. She could not sit still or get calm no matter how hard she tried. She began having frightening panic attacks. Her anxiety became so out of control that she could barely go to school. Her mother took her to see a mental health professional, who taught her relaxation techniques that quiet down the mind and body. Deep breathing was one of these calmative practices. Indeed, deep breathing, combined with other relaxation tools, empowered her to better manage stress. As she proudly explains:

> I was in school one day and the teacher had given us an assignment and normally I would have gotten nervous because we had to finish it by the end of the period and that was something that was triggering for me. I used the breathing exercises 'cause I felt myself getting worked up so I told myself it's okay, I can deal with this, I am capable. And where normally I would have not been able to control my anxiety, I did, and I realized it was working. It made me want to work harder and learn more tools so I could continue to get better.[17]

Relaxing Breaths

As Jackie learned, there are many ways to relax the body and mind, which help counteract the effects of stress. Breathing deeply, slowly, and rhythmically is one of the most effective ways. When people are stressed, they breathe rapidly and shallowly, up in their chest. Their shoulders rise slightly, and their stomach does not move in and out. Fast, shallow breathing prevents sufficient oxygen from getting into the body and enough carbon dioxide from getting out of it. This imbalance can make individuals feel confused, dizzy, breathless, and even more stressed. Conversely, when people are relaxed, they tend to breathe from their diaphragm, a muscle that separates the chest from the abdomen. Relaxed breathing is deep and slow. Slow, deep breathing allows the body to take in more oxygen and expel more carbon dioxide. When the correct balance of oxygen and carbon dioxide in the body is maintained, dizzy, confused, and breathless feelings subside. In addition, deep breathing turns off the fight-or-flight response. It signals the brain to release chemicals that inhibit the production and release of stress hormones. As a result, blood pressure and heart rate decrease, brain activity calms, and people feel tranquil and relaxed.

Deep breathing involves consciously breathing slowly, deeply, and rhythmically from your diaphragm. Certain breathing exercises can teach you how to do this. One of the simplest is known as sigh breathing. To sigh breathe, inhale deeply through your nose, silently count to three, then exhale slowly through your mouth almost like you are sighing. Another breathing exercise helps make you more aware of where you are breathing from. In this exercise, you relax your stomach and put one hand below your ribs on your diaphragm. Then you inhale slowly through your nose, focusing on your diaphragm rising, hold the breath for three seconds, then exhale slowly through your mouth, focusing on your diaphragm lowering.

Breathing exercises are so effective that US Navy SEALs are trained to use a method known as tactical or box breathing to

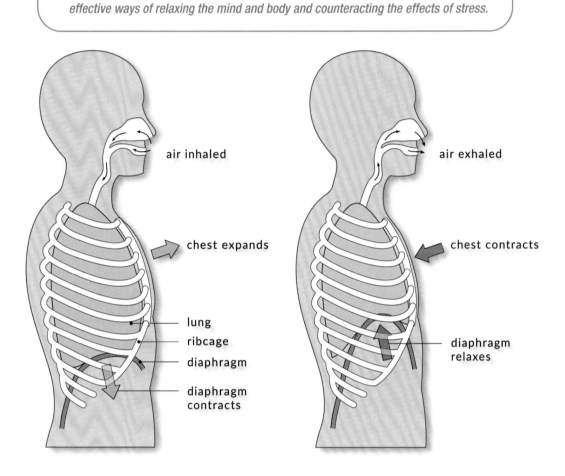

Breathing deeply, slowly, and rhythmically from the diaphragm is one of the most effective ways of relaxing the mind and body and counteracting the effects of stress.

air inhaled

chest expands

lung

ribcage

diaphragm

diaphragm
contracts

air exhaled

chest contracts

diaphragm
relaxes

gain calm and mental control during stressful events. To breathe like a SEAL, inhale for four seconds, hold your breath for four seconds, exhale for four seconds, hold your breath for four seconds, then repeat. There are many other breathing exercises.

Whether you make deep breathing exercises a daily practice or just take a few deep breaths right before tackling a stressful task, a number of studies have shown that deep breathing really does help counteract stress. One of the best things about deep breathing is that you can do it anywhere and at any time, standing, sitting, or lying down. You can combine it with stretching, yoga, or meditation. Or you can breathe deeply at your school desk before taking a test without anyone knowing that you are doing so. As fifteen-year-old Sadie explains, "Breathing is like the simplest thing in the world—you can't not do it. But I never realized how I breathe can make such a difference in how I feel."[18]

Developing Mindfulness

Breathing exercises help divert your attention from stressful thoughts and focus it on your breath, which helps in the development of mindfulness. When people are overly stressed or anxious, they often feel like they cannot control their thoughts. Their minds tend to dwell on negative thoughts about things they cannot change or control, such as events that happened in the past or that might happen in the future. Practicing mindfulness helps you detach from negative thoughts and focus on the here and now. Mindfulness practice combines breathing and meditation. It has a physiological effect on the body, which helps you relax mentally and physically. Mindfulness practice has been shown to inhibit the release of cortisol, decrease pain, and lower anxiety, depression, and impulsive behavior. And it improves overall mental well-being. Imaging studies have shown that over time, practicing mindfulness causes visible changes to regions of the brain involved in emotions, learning, the ability to focus, and memory. These changes improve the ability to think clearly and make better decisions when faced with a stressful situation.

> "Breathing is like the simplest thing in the world—you can't not do it. But I never realized how I breathe can make such a difference in how I feel."[18]
>
> —Sadie, teen

Mindfulness exercises focus on staying in the present moment and observing your feelings and thoughts without judging or reacting to them. Once learned, mindfulness makes it easier for you to tune out troubling thoughts by shifting your attention away from them and onto something else. This has a calming effect. It takes practice to develop mindfulness skills, since your mind may tend to wander. But it is worth the effort. As a teen named Nicole R. explains on the Mindfulness for Teens website:

> Before learning about mindfulness and practicing it, I had not realized how much of my life I was living outside of the present moment. I am a very anxious person, and I'm often worrying about the future or the past. Mindfulness has allowed me to live more in the now. I feel a sense of self-awareness that I didn't have before, and it has been incredibly useful for managing my anxiety. . . . I think that mindfulness can benefit everyone. In the beginning, you may feel silly or find it hard, but it will get easier. You just have to approach it with an open mind and no expectations. . . . The hardest part is getting yourself to do it. The next hardest part is getting yourself to stick with it. Everything else is much easier.[19]

Mindfulness can be practiced through both structured and unstructured exercises. And there are many websites and apps to help guide you. One of the simplest structured exercises involves

Practicing mindfulness helps you detach from negative thoughts and focus on the here and now.

Doing things to pamper yourself can help you feel less stressed. Taking a warm bath in a softly lit room with peaceful music playing in the background, for example, is very soothing. Warm water, soft lighting, and soft music all have a relaxing effect on the mind and body. Adding a bath bomb and/or bath salts in a sweet-smelling, calming scent enhances the effect, as does lighting an aromatherapy candle. When you are finished soaking, put on your softest, coziest, most comfortable clothes and do something restful like working a puzzle or reading.

Getting a massage—whether full body or just your neck, feet, or hands—is also extremely relaxing, especially if calmative essential oils are used in the treatment. One type of massage, known as a Swedish massage, involves the application of gentle strokes and can be very beneficial. Some licensed massage therapists make house calls. Others offer their services in day spas and gyms. If you are a member of a gym that has a sauna or steam room, take advantage of these amenities. The heat can relieve muscle tension, relax you, and lessen stress.

focusing on your breathing. To get started, choose a quiet location and a time in which you can practice for at least five minutes each day without interruption. When you are ready, sit on a chair or on the floor with your arms relaxed and your back straight. You should feel comfortable, because you want to remain still. Close your eyes, breathe normally, relax, and notice how the air feels against your skin and how the chair or floor feels against your body. Then focus your attention on your breathing without trying to control it. Notice the rhythm and pace of your breathing and how inhaling and exhaling make you feel. If a distracting thought interrupts your focus, notice what is happening and whisper "not now" or any word or short phrase that redirects you. Let the thought waft away, and refocus on your breath.

> "I am a very anxious person, and I'm often worrying about the future or the past. Mindfulness has allowed me to live more in the now."[19]
>
> —Nicole R., teen

If sitting still is difficult for you, you can practice walking meditation, another structured mindfulness exercise. To do this, find a quiet place to walk slowly. As you walk, draw your attention to the physical act of walking and how it feels to stand, move forward, and stay balanced. Notice how the air feels as it touches your face. As before, if distracting thoughts pop into your head, whisper "not now" and refocus on walking.

You can do less structured mindfulness techniques anywhere and at any time. Most involve focusing on your senses. For instance, while eating try to concentrate on the food, how it looks, and how it feels as you chew it, and follow it down as you swallow. Notice the aroma, texture, and color. Once again, if your mind wanders, whisper "not now" and redirect your attention. You can focus on sounds, tactile sensations, sights, and/or smells in a similar manner. You can even practice mindfulness while doing routine activities like brushing your teeth. And you can be mindful outdoors, too. In fact, research shows that practicing mindfulness outdoors is very beneficial. For example, try going out into your backyard or to a park and really looking at a flower. Take in the color, the scent, and the way the stem, petals, and leaves feel. Or walk on a beach while focusing on the sounds of the waves. No matter what mindfulness techniques you practice, once you have mastered the skills involved, you should be better able to manage stress and anxiety.

Progressive Muscle Relaxation

Progressive muscle relaxation is another technique that helps you relax and better manage stress and anxiety. When the body's fight-or-flight response is activated, your muscles become tense and ready for action. Once the stress passes, the muscles relax. However, if you suffer from chronic stress, your muscles remain tense. Tense muscles are a common symptom of anxiety. Chronically tense muscles cause pain and muscle cramps. Pain is a common stress trigger. It makes it difficult to relax or sleep. And it can add to your anxiety. As anxiety levels increase, so does muscle tension, which can then lead to a painful cycle.

Progressive muscle relaxation is a strategy that helps break this cycle. It loosens tense muscles and eases anxiety. Pro-

Research has shown that spending time in nature has a number of positive effects on an individual's well-being. It can help relax you, relieve stress and anxiety, improve your mood, and boost feelings of contentment. The American Heart Association recommends a number of relaxing outdoor activities that can help lessen stress and anxiety. These include going outdoors and watching a sunrise or sunset or sitting on a hilltop and looking at the scenery. Taking a walk in the woods is another, as is reading or studying in nature. In fact, research suggests studying in a natural environment can improve memory and problem-solving ability.

Having a picnic can also be relaxing, especially if you do so with a close friend. Going camping can also be peaceful. It allows you to disconnect from everyday life, especially if you turn off your phone and stay off social media. If you are lucky enough to be camping near a natural hot spring, consider taking a soak. Many natural hot springs contain minerals with calmative and healing properties.

gressive muscle relaxation involves tightening different muscles groups, then releasing the tension. It is easy to learn and simple to do. You can start with any muscle group, but most practitioners start with the lower extremities and work their way up to the face. To get started, lie down on a comfortable surface with your arms at your sides and your legs about shoulder width apart. Close your eyes and take a few deep breaths. Next, breathing normally, tightly curl your toes and hold for five seconds. Release the tension by uncurling your toes, and relax for ten seconds. As you release the tension, concentrate on how relaxed your toes feel. Repeat the procedure, working up from your calf muscles to your thighs, followed by your buttocks, abdomen, chest, and shoulders. Next, tense and relax your hands and fingers, then move to your neck, lips, nose, and eyes. When you are finished, lie still and breathe naturally as you enjoy the way your body feels.

To help enhance the effect of progressive muscle relaxation, many people combine it with visualization exercises. Visualization is a technique in which people envision mental images of a particular goal. For example, as you tighten then release each muscle or muscle group, imagine the tension in that muscle group flowing out of you and floating away, like a soap bubble. And as you lie still at the end of the exercise, visualize yourself in a serene and beautiful place where you are free of stress and pain. An added benefit of visualization is that over time, visualizing this serene stress-free place can help you relax even if it is not paired with progressive relaxation therapy.

Relaxing Scents

Other relaxation strategies involve the sense of smell. It is the most powerful of all the senses. Scents have been shown to trigger memories and emotions. Different scents have different effects on the mind and body. Using scents as a form of therapy is known as aromatherapy.

Aromatherapy involves using essential oils extracted from plants to promote wellness. Typically, the oil is put in a special diffuser, which circulates it into the air as a mist. Inhaling the mist sends it into the bloodstream and to the brain via the lungs and olfactory nerves. Different essential oils have different properties. Some oils contain chemicals that have a calming effect. These include lavender, chamomile, sandalwood, clary sage, and geranium oils, among others. Lavender oil in particular has been shown

The scent of lavender is particularly effective at calming the mind and body and reducing feelings of stress and anxiety.

to be especially soothing. It appears to ease stress and anxiety, improve mood, lower blood pressure, and promote sleep. When the scent is inhaled, a substance in lavender oil activates nerves in the nose. These nerves signal the brain to release GABA, a chemical that blocks the brain from sending stress-related messages to the body. This calms the mind and body and lessens feelings of stress and anxiety. A Turkish study reported by the U.S. National Institute of Health found that inhaling the scent of lavender oil helped patients in intensive care feel less anxious.

If you do not like the scent of lavender, you can still get stress relief using other calming essential oils. What particular oil you use depends on your personal preference. You can also blend calming oils together or purchase ready-made calming blends. And you can combine aromatherapy with other relaxing activities to supercharge the stress-busting effect. For instance, listening to soft music while practicing aromatherapy is very relaxing, and so is adding a few drops of essential oil to a warm bath. You can also combine progressive muscle relaxation with aromatherapy or practice mindfulness by focusing on the scent of an essential oil. Using visualization with aromatherapy is another de-stressor. To do so, as you inhale, imagine the oil molecules entering and spreading through your body and calming you.

> "In our stressful and often negative world, your decision to make relaxing a priority will help you navigate, handle, and minimize stress."[20]
>
> —Susan C. Young, author and motivational speaker

What is most important in managing stress is not what relaxation techniques you practice but that you allow yourself to recharge and relax. "Relaxing can bring relief to much of what ails you," says Wisconsin author and motivational speaker Susan C. Young. "In our stressful and often negative world, your decision to make relaxing a priority will help you navigate, handle, and minimize stress. Doing so will positively impact your health, well-being, and happiness."[20]

CHAPTER FOUR

Taking Control

Sam is a young artist who has battled anxiety since he was thirteen years old. Over the years, he has experienced fear, panic attacks, and health issues related to anxiety. On occasion anxiety and stress have kept him from doing things he wanted to do and negatively affected the quality of his life. He says, "Everyday activities can trigger stress in me, especially if there is a deadline and I feel that I can't meet the deadline or requirement. A lot of times it comes with low self-esteem. If I feel that I'm not capable or well equipped to do something I get stressed out about that. I like to feel that I am in control, which is part of my anxiety."[21]

It is impossible to control everything in life. However, by using stress management techniques that focus on the way you interact with the world, improve how you view yourself, or involve getting emotional support, individuals can gain greater control over stress and anxiety.

Time Management

Like Sam, many young people struggle with meeting deadlines. Most teens have very busy schedules. Paige, a Philadelphia high school junior, is a good example. She attends school from 8:00 a.m. until 2:30 p.m. After school, she volunteers at a neighborhood youth center. Then she rushes off to dance lessons. She also frequently attends club meetings and play rehearsals. Often she does not arrive back home until 9:00 p.m. and is up until well past midnight doing homework and studying. Even during the COVID-19 pandemic, her schedule has been loaded with online classes and Zoom meetings.

Paige's schedule is not unusual. Not surprisingly, fitting everything in and getting everything done in a timely fashion stresses her. She is not alone. It is not unusual for teens to have three hours of homework each night, in addition to attending school and participating in extracurricular activities. Many teens feel like there is not enough time to do all things they have to do, let alone the things they want to do. Moreover, they often put off large projects because they feel intimidated by their size. Consequently, they often feel overwhelmed. Using time management skills helps them gain more control over their lives, which helps relieve stress and anxiety.

Time management is about planning and taking control of the time you spend on different activities. It involves a variety of strategies. Prioritizing what needs to be done and in what order is one of these strategies. To do this, make a list of all the things you have to do or want to do in a set time period. This can be a day, week, month, or semester. Include schoolwork, appointments, chores, and extracurricular and social activities. When applicable, add the date when each task must be completed. Now examine your list and assign each item a letter from A to C based on its importance, with A being the most urgent and C being the least. Finally, rank the tasks within each category based on their importance. For instance, if you have three A items, you would rank them A1, A2, and A3, and then do the same with the other letters. You now have a prioritized list of what you need to do and in what order, starting with A1 and ending with the last C item. This helps get you organized and keeps you on track so that you tackle each item in the appropriate time. As a result, you should feel less stressed. You can use a calendar, app, or planner to help keep you organized.

Another strategy helps with big, daunting tasks like a term paper by breaking the task down into smaller more manageable chunks. It's easy to get overwhelmed by large projects.

Using time management tools such as online calendars can help reduce stress and anxiety.

The stress can make you procrastinate, which can raise your stress level even more. To keep this from happening, try listing the different things you must do to get the project done in the order they must be performed. Then tackle each small task one-by-one until the project is complete. For example, for a history paper, your first task might be to reread a chapter in your textbook, taking notes on important details. The next task might be to find information about the subject on a particular website, and so on. Even include tasks like buying a report cover on the list, so that you are not hit with any delaying surprises. Understanding the various steps that must be performed to get a large task done and tackling each item one at a time makes the task less daunting and stressful.

In fact, once you begin to manage your time more effectively, you should have more time to do things that you enjoy. However, try not to let time-wasting activities such as playing video games, going on social media, or flipping TV channels suck up all your time. Set a reasonable limit on how much time you spend on these types of activities, and set the timer on your cell phone to remind you when it is time to stop. That way you can enjoy these activities without letting them interfere with the things that you must complete.

Being More Assertive

Many teens feel that they have little control over their lives. They feel stressed because they take on tasks and activities that they would rather not do or that interfere with things that they need to do. Or they feel pushed around and mistreated by others but refrain from speaking up for themselves. Stress and anxiety can make it difficult for individuals to assert themselves, share their feelings, or say no when something is against their best interest. This is because anxious thoughts can make you worry about what others might think of you if you express an opinion or speak up for yourself. Anxious thoughts can make you imagine dreadful consequences—such as losing a friendship, job, relationship, or position on a team—if you say the wrong thing or do not defer to others. As Oregon author and mental health counselor Tanya J. Peterson explains, "Anxious thoughts and emotions interfere in how we experience ourselves, others, and the world around us."[22]

Although it is admirable to put the needs of others above your own, if you bottle up your feelings and rarely assert yourself, your needs are often ignored. This can make you feel like you have no control over your life and that others do not care about or respect you. But this is not true. Realistically, it is almost impossible for others to know what you want or need if you do not tell them. Nevertheless, bottling up your needs can make you feel resentful and anxious. According to Peterson, "Being passive actually increases anxiety. . . . You have

> "Anxious thoughts and emotions interfere in how we experience ourselves, others, and the world around us."[22]
>
> —Tanya J. Peterson, author and mental health counselor

43

Many teens who experience overwhelming stress or anxiety are ashamed to admit they have a problem. Often they feel alone and abnormal, when actually, they are neither. People of all ages and ethnicities, including many celebrities, have experienced similar issues. In an effort to lend their support to these teens, many of these celebrities have spoken out. Ariana Grande, for example, has been very open about her experiences dealing with anxiety, depression, and PTSD. Her hit song "Breathin" touches on her struggle with anxiety. Similarly, some of Billie Eilish's songs reference her battle with anxiety and depression. In an interview with *Rolling Stone*, the teen singer-songwriter openly admitted to struggling with panic attacks. Other young celebrities who have talked about their battles with stress and anxiety include Shawn Mendes, Selena Gomez, Lana Condor, and Zayn Malik, among many others. These celebrities want teens battling stress and anxiety to know that they are not alone and should not be ashamed of their feelings.

legitimate needs, but anxiety makes you reluctant to speak up for them. However, when those real needs aren't met, stress and anxiety increase, making you more anxious."[23]

Conversely, sharing what you think or feel in a calm and respectful manner helps you get your needs met, which lessens stress and anxiety. However, becoming more assertive is not easy for anxious individuals because you are acting in a way that ordinarily stresses you. But by asserting yourself in small ways at first, you can start to gain more control. For example, if you have a test to study for and your bestie wants to spend the evening texting with you, rather than letting yourself be distracted and lose valuable time (which will only add to your stress), it is okay to tell your friend that you have to study and can only chat for five minutes. Despite what anxiety may be telling you to the contrary, it is highly unlikely that your best friend will end your relationship because you communicated your needs.

Once you begin asserting yourself in small ways, you should gain more self-assurance, feel less stressed, and be more able to stand up for yourself on bigger issues. To help you express your feelings about bigger issues, it may help you to write down what you want to say and practice saying it in front of a mirror. This may sound silly, but it can boost your confidence and lower your fear and tension.

And whether issues are major or minor, try not to confuse being assertive with being aggressive. When people are assertive, they express their thoughts, feelings, and opinions in a calm, courteous, and respectful manner. When people are aggressive, they may be rude, insulting, or violent, which is not how you want to come across. As Peterson explains, "Think of the process of becoming more assertive, less passive, as personal growth that will ultimately decrease anxiety as you become more comfortable with yourself and others. You can still be the kind and considerate person you are. You'll simply be standing beside others rather than under their feet."[24]

Calmly and respectfully telling someone you know that you need to concentrate on studying is unlikely to spoil a friendship and will help prevent the stress of falling behind in your schoolwork.

Because so many young people experience academic stress, many high schools and colleges have taken steps to help reduce student stress and anxiety. Almost all high schools employ school counselors. They are trained mental health professionals. Students who are overwhelmed by stress can gain help and support by talking with them. In addition, some high schools have introduced classroom lessons in mindfulness therapy and provide time within the school day for students to practice it.

Colleges, too, are helping young people gain more control. They offer student health centers, where students can get assistance dealing with physical and emotional health issues. In addition, some colleges have established stress-free zones. Typically, these are quiet outdoor spaces where students can read and play games. Some colleges allow students to bring emotional support animals to class. Kent State University in Ohio brings therapy dogs on campus for stressed-out students to cuddle with, and Dalhousie University in Halifax, Nova Scotia, set up a puppy room for just this purpose. Taking advantage of these services helps students gain more control over their emotions.

Fighting Perfectionism

Many teens think they have to do everything perfectly. However, this is an impossible feat. By demanding perfection of themselves, individuals set themselves up for failure because they cannot live up to their own unrealistic goals and expectations. Consequently, their self-esteem drops, and they often feel hopeless. Not surprisingly, perfectionism is a common source of stress. Sam admits to having this problem. He explains, "Something I deal with all the time, especially related to my creative artwork, is that I feel that it's not good enough; it could be better, and therefore, personally, I could be better. It definitely creates some anxiety and negative feelings towards myself."[25]

Indeed, while trying to do your best is healthy, perfectionism is not. It can interfere with many aspects of life. It can cause you to repeatedly redo an assignment even if you have already done a fine job. As a result, you may fail to complete the assignment on time or at all. Plus, this behavior keeps you from tackling the next thing on your to-do list in a timely manner, all of which adds to the pressure and stress you are putting on yourself.

Insisting on being the best at everything can also keep individuals from trying new things, participating in fun activities, or meeting new people out of fear of making a mistake or not being good enough. Making matters worse, perfectionists tend to be their own worst critic. When perfectionists make mistakes, they tend to view even the teeniest error as a huge failure and a reflection on themselves. As a consequence, they think less of themselves. And they think that others will judge them poorly and think less of them because they are not perfect. This kind of thinking is very stressful. Australian author, podcaster, and mental health counselor Rachael Kable, who battled anxiety and perfectionism during her teen years, recalls:

> I'll never forget the time I failed my first driving test. I was so stressed about doing everything perfectly that I couldn't think straight and made a simple error. When I found out that I'd failed, it felt like the end of the world. I thought everyone would be judging me and I told myself I was a loser and I kept imagining what I should have done differently. I didn't want to tell anyone what had happened because I was so ashamed of myself.[26]

Kable eventually realized the futility of trying to be perfect. Although she still tries to do her best, she no longer judges herself so harshly. She used a number of strategies to keep perfectionism from controlling her, including positive self-talk.

Positive self-talk can help you change perfectionist behavior, thereby keeping the stress and anxiety it leads to at bay. The first step is to recognize your perfectionist thoughts and behaviors. Next, try to reframe these thoughts. Remind yourself that it is okay to make mistakes and that it is impossible to be perfect all the time. Tell yourself that making mistakes is part of life and a way to learn. Then, think back to times you made mistakes or did not quite measure up and how little effect these actions had on your life. Finally, give yourself permission to try new things just for fun. At first it may help to do this activity in a safe environment with someone you trust to keep you from feeling judged. For example, before performing karaoke solo at a big party, begin by performing as part of a group at a small gathering of your closest friends.

Getting Support

Often when teens are overwhelmed by stress and anxiety, they do not let anyone know that they are having problems, because they want to seem capable and independent. However, keeping these issues secret is stressful. But getting emotional support by talking about your concerns with caring and trusted friends, adults, or a mental health professional can help you gain more control. These people can serve as your support network. They can provide a sympathetic ear and help you feel that you are not alone. Actress Skai Jackson, for example, has battled stress and anxiety for

Spending time with family and friends can help improve your mental and physical well-being.

many years. She depends on her close friends to help her when she feels overwhelmed. "My friends are my everything," she says. "When I feel that anxiety, I always call them or text them, and they talk me through it. . . . My friends know I deal with a lot of things, especially anxiety, and they're always here for me, which is amazing."[27]

In addition to your peers, you can find support among family members, teachers, religious leaders, and other adults you trust. But remember, support is not a one-way thing. To strengthen your relationships, you, too, need to be supportive of the members of your network. If you are there for your friends and family members when they are hav-

> "My friends are my everything. When I feel that anxiety, I always call them or text them, and they talk me through it."[27]
>
> —Skai Jackson, actress

ing problems, your relationship will strengthen and grow. Spending time with friends and family members in your support network also strengthens your connection and level of trust. Not only does having these connections and this network help you feel more in control, having strong connections with others has been shown to improve people's mental and physical well-being.

Joining a support group can also provide emotional support. Support groups are made up of people who share a common problem. Members share their experiences, swap healthy coping strategies, and provide each other with encouragement. There are free online and local support groups that focus on anxiety and stress management. Some are especially for young people. As a matter of fact, the COVID-19 pandemic has increased the number of online anxiety support groups. There are even online teen group therapy sessions for young people battling anxiety. These are led by mental health professionals and specially trained teen counselors. Many of these groups charge a small fee per session and accept health insurance.

Some people prefer one-on-one online counseling from a licensed mental health professional such as a psychologist, psychiatrist, medical doctor, social worker, or mental health counselor. These individuals are trained to help people cope with overwhelming stress and anxiety. In addition to providing a safe, nonjudgmental space to talk about problems, they help patients identify stressors and provide them with coping strategies. Often they administer a treatment known as cognitive behavioral therapy. This type of therapy helps individuals become more aware of how negative thoughts contribute to stress and anxiety and provides the tools to confront these thoughts. In some cases mental health professionals may prescribe antianxiety medications such as Xanax or Ativan or antidepressants such as Zoloft to relieve anxiety symptoms.

> "Far from being a sign of weakness, owning our struggles and taking the steps to heal is powerful."[28]
>
> —Camila Cabello, singer-songwriter

No one has to let stress control his or her life. There are many paths a person can take and many strategies that can be used to help manage stress and anxiety. As singer-songwriter Camila Cabello, who battles severe anxiety, explains, "Far from being a sign of weakness, owning our struggles and taking the steps to heal is powerful."[28]

SOURCE NOTES

Introduction: A Stressful Time

1. Quoted in Lauren Rearick, "Willow Smith and Tyler Cole Create Anxiety-Themed Art Exhibit Before New Album," *Teen Vogue*, March 11, 2020. www.teenvogue.com.
2. Elizabeth Scott, "How to Cope with Stress and Become More Resilient," Verywell Mind, November 19, 2019. www.verywellmind.com.

Chapter One: Not Just an Emotional Issue

3. Quoted in *Choices*, "Living with Anxiety," February 2020. https://choices.scholastic.com.
4. Karen Young, "Anxiety in Teens—How to Help a Teenager Deal with Anxiety," Hey Sigmund, 2020. www.heysigmund.com.
5. Quoted in Michelle Crouch, "Tame the Stress Monster," *Choices*, September 2018. https://choices.scholastic.com.
6. Julia Michaels, "'Issues' Singer Julia Michaels on Living with Anxiety: 'It's like You're in a Prison with Yourself,'" *Glamour*, January 24, 2019. www.glamour.com.
7. Quoted in Jenny McCoy, "If You're Waking Up with Anxiety, You're Not Alone," *Glamour*, June 3, 2020. www.glamour.com.
8. Quoted in Josh Smith, "As Enola Holmes Drops on Netflix, GLAMOUR Digital Cover Star Millie Bobby Brown Opens Up About Anxiety, Growing Up in the Public Eye & Her Marriage Hopes for Eleven," *Glamour*, August 28, 2020. www.glamourmagazine.co.uk.
9. Quoted in Smith, "As Enola Holmes Drops on Netflix, GLAMOUR Digital Cover Star Millie Bobby Brown Opens Up About Anxiety, Growing Up in the Public Eye & Her Marriage Hopes for Eleven."

10. Quoted in Jenny McCoy, "26 Inspirational Mental Health Quotes," *Glamour*, September 30, 2020. www.glamour.com.

Chapter Two: Fighting Stress with a Healthy Lifestyle

11. Rizza Bermio-Gonzalez, "How Your Diet Affects Your Anxiety," *Treating Anxiety* (blog), HealthyPlace, August 11, 2020. www.healthyplace.com.
12. Elizabeth Scott, "Caffeine, Stress and Your Health," Verywell Mind, January 17, 2020. www.verywellmind.com.
13. Tanya J. Peterson, "List of Foods That Help and Hurt Anxiety," HealthyPlace, June 18, 2019. www.healthyplace.com.
14. Quoted in Kelsey Calderon, "When You Drink Hot Water Every Day, This Is What Happens to Your Body," The List, August 20, 2020. www.thelist.com.
15. Quoted in Tom McGrath, "Teenagers Are More Stressed than Ever. Who's to Blame?," *Philadelphia*, February 4, 2019. www.phillymag.com.
16. Quoted in Rebecca Aydin and Sherin Shibu, "It's International Stress Awareness Week—Here's How Michelle Obama, Bill Gates, and Other Leaders Handle Stressful Situations," Insider, November 6, 2019. www.insider.com.

Chapter Three: Relax and Recharge

17. Quoted in Child Mind Institute, "How Jackie Got Her Life Back," 2021. https://childmind.org.
18. Quoted in Earl Hipp, *Fighting Invisible Tigers*. Minneapolis, MN: Free Spirit, 2019, p. 38.
19. Nicole R., "Youth Voices," Mindfulness for Teens. http://mindfulnessforteens.com.
20. Quoted in Goodreads, "Stress Management Quotes," 2021. www.goodreads.com.

Chapter Four: Taking Control

21. Sam, telephone interview with the author, November 17, 2020.
22. Tanya J. Peterson, "Does Anxiety Make You Too Passive? Stop Being a Doormat," *Anxiety-Schmanxiety* (blog), HealthyPlace, July 2, 2020. www.healthyplace.com.

23. Tanya J. Peterson, "Anxiety and Assertiveness: Four Tips," *Anxiety-Schmanxiety* (blog), HealthyPlace, September 18, 2014. www.healthyplace.com.
24. Tanya J. Peterson, "Does Anxiety Make You Too Passive?"
25. Sam, interview.
26. Rachael Kable, "How Perfectionism Perpetuates Stress (and What to Do About It)," *Rachael's Blog*. www.rachaelkable .com.
27. Quoted in Atahabih Germain, "I'm Trying to Break Myself Out of It': Skai Jackson Opens Up About Her Struggle with Anxiety," Atlanta Black Star, October 20, 2020. https://atlanta blackstar.com.
28. Quoted in Gianluca Russo, "Camila Cabello Opened Up About OCD and Anxiety in a Personal Essay," *Teen Vogue*, May 30, 2020. www.teenvogue.com.

WHERE TO GET HELP

Hotlines and Call Centers

Boys Town National Hotline

www.boystown.org

Boys Town is an organization that provides health services to youths and families. Counselors offer 24/7 crisis intervention and short-term counseling. Referrals to community resources are offered. Call toll-free (800) 448-3000 or text: VOICE to 20121.

Crisis Text Line

www.crisistextline.org

The Crisis Text Line provides text-based counseling for mental health issues, including anxiety, stress, and depression. Text: HOME to 741741.

National Suicide Prevention Lifeline

https://suicidepreventionlifeline.org

The National Suicide Prevention Lifeline is a network of crisis centers that offers 24/7 counseling and emotional support to people in any type of emotional distress. Counselors can be reached via telephone or through online chat on the website. Call toll-free (800) 273-8255.

Teen Line

https://teenlineonline.org/

Teen Line is a California-based group that provides free peer-based emotional support to teens throughout the United States from 6:00 p.m. to 10:00 p.m. Pacific Standard Time. It can be reached via telephone, text, and email. A message board on the website allows users to hold discussions and ask questions. Call toll-free (800) 852-8336 or text: TEEN to 839863.

Helpful Apps

AntiStress Anxiety Relief Game

Available for: iPhone and Android
Price: Free

This antistress app offers games and activities designed to provide fun distractions and short-term relief from stress.

Breathwrk

Available for: iPhone
Price: Free

Breathwrk provides a variety of breathing exercises with instructions. Different exercises focus on either relieving stress, becoming energized, or promoting relaxation and sleep.

My Homework Student Planner

Available for: iPhone and Android
Price: Free

My Homework Student Planner is a virtual planner that helps students become more organized and manage their time. It tracks assignments, classes, and tests; sends due date reminders; and can be synced between different devices.

Smiling Mind

Available for: iPhone and Android
Price: Free

Smiling Mind was developed by psychologists and educators. It provides hundreds of daily meditation and mindfulness exercises with special programs for teens.

ORGANIZATIONS AND WEBSITES

American Academy of Child & Adolescent Psychiatry (AACAP)

www.aacap.org

The AACAP is an organization dedicated to educating the public about mental health issues affecting young people. A search on the website yields lots of information about managing anxiety and anxiety disorders.

American Institute of Stress

www.stress.org

The American Institute of Stress aims to help people learn about stress and how to manage it. It offers many articles, free magazines, and a blog, among other information.

Anxiety and Depression Association of America (ADAA)

www.adaa.org

The ADAA is an organization committed to helping people with anxiety, anxiety disorders, and depression. It offers information about anxiety, tips on how to manage stress and anxiety, and online support groups. It also helps people locate mental health professionals and mental health apps.

Child Mind Institute

www.childmind.org

The Child Mind Institute is dedicated to improving the mental health of children and adolescents. It provides a variety of articles and information about anxiety on its website, including information about anxiety and the coronavirus.

National Institute of Mental Health (NIMH)

www.nimh.nih.gov

The NIMH works to improve mental health and reduce mental illness through scientific research. It offers information about stress, stress reduction, and anxiety disorders on its website.

TeensHealth

www.teenshealth.org

This website contains lots of information for teens about coping with stress. It also provides information about relaxation strategies and offers videos, articles, and teen stories.

FOR FURTHER RESEARCH

Books

Jodi Aman, *Anxiety . . . I'm So Done with You: A Teen's Guide to Ditching Toxic Stress and Hardwiring Your Brain for Happiness*. New York: Skyhorse, 2020.

Tammy Gagne, *Teens and Anxiety*. San Diego: Reference-Point Press, 2021.

Shannon Harts, *Stress and Anxiety*. New York: Rosen, 2021.

Dawn Huebner, *Outsmarting Worry*. London: Jessica Kingsley, 2018.

Celina McManus, *Understanding Anxiety*. San Diego: BrightPoint, 2021.

Internet Sources

Astrid Eira, "32 Student Stress Statistics in 2020: Bullying, Mental Health & Gun Violence," Finances Online, 2021. https://financesonline.com.

Kylie Gilbert, "Feeling Anxious Is the New Normal. Here's When You Should Be Concerned," *InStyle*, September 1, 2020. www.instyle.com.

Help Guide, "Stress Symptoms, Signs, and Causes." www.helpguide.org.

National Center for Complementary and Integrative Health, "Mind and Body Approaches for Stress and Anxiety: What the Science Says," 2020. www.nccih.nih.gov.

Dzung Vo, "Guided Meditations," Mindfulness for Teens. http://mindfulnessforteens.com.

INDEX

PICTURE CREDITS

ABOUT THE AUTHOR

Barbara Sheen is the author of 108 books for young people. She lives in New Mexico with her family. In her spare time she likes to swim, garden, walk, cook, and read.